The Smart & Easy Guide To Crafts That Sell: How To Build A Crafting Home Business And Find Hobbies That Make Money

Mary J. Hubert

Legal Stuff

Table of Contents

Introduction

Do you have an eye for detail? Are you sensitive to things you need and creative enough to make them out of bits and pieces and odds and ends? You are a crafter!

Do you like making personalized items to give away as gifts? Do your friends often tell you that they love the personalized gifts you've given them because they get good use out of those gifts? You are a talented crafter!

Do you have patience and perseverance? Can you stick to a task and see it through? Can you think out of the box and tweak common things until they become sellable items? You may very well be a budding crafting entrepreneur!

People tell you that you must do what you love and love what you do. People always say that if you do this, work becomes fun. For most people who find themselves employed, they are doing what they need to do in order to survive. They cultivate hobbies in their spare time to give themselves an outlet for the creative energy that their day job does not give them opportunity to express.

Then again, there are some people who have taken their hobbies one step, or maybe a few more small steps further and they are actually earning income from their hobbies. Crafters often make money from their crafting hobbies. You could be one of those crafters.

This book presumes that you are already a good crafter. You are dedicated to what you do because you have a drive for personal excellence. Your crafted products speak highly of who you are because you are committed to doing your best and doing it efficiently.

This book, then, already presumes that you have a crafting hobby and that you have the talent to create sellable items. This book will help you take your hobby (the work that you love) and make it work for you so that it will become an occupation and a stable source of income.

In order to build a successful business out of a hobby, there must be an investment of your time, your undivided attention and your creative juices. The book presumes that you have already decided to make this investment. This book will assist you by giving you pointers on how to make your crafting hobby an income-generating hobby that may, with perseverance and luck, become a going concern and business venture.

Wanted: original ideas

You need originality and focus. You can always find a best-selling item, copy it, sell it and make some money from it. You can always do that – countless others do that everyday. But then, if you stick to that plan of action, you will not be setting a market trend, you will be tripping over yourself trying to follow trends that others set for you. If this is what you want, then by all means, do it.

But if you have bigger brighter dreams of finding something you are truly good at and something that people will take notice, find interesting enough to purchase and be happy to use, then you are not simply looking for a source of income, you are looking for a source of entrepreneurial satisfaction and fulfillment. This is the motivation that will take your sideline into mainstream. This kind of motivation will keep you on your tippy toes and working long after all others in your league have thrown in the towel.

The goal then is not only to make money from a hobby but to find fulfillment and satisfaction in turning a hobby into an income-generating business concern. In doing this, you contribute not only to your own personal wealth you also contribute to your family income and even support your country's drive toward economic recovery. If you succeed in making your hobby a business, you will provide employment for others. If your entrepreneurial drive is particularly infectious, you can inspire others to also become entrepreneurs and empower them to find their own source of income and entrepreneurial satisfaction.

What this book talks about

Let's say that you have decided to make your hobby a profitable business from your own home. What should you do first? How can you go about it? This book is dedicated to helping you realize this dream. It will teach you basic market research, product development and marketing techniques that you can apply to turn your crafting hobby into a veritable source of income and entrepreneurial satisfaction.

First Things First: What's Your Business Concept?

Most people think that if you haven't yet thought up a name for your business, it's the most logical starting point. In order to come up with an appropriate name, though, you need a business concept. A business concept is a brief description of your company and what it intends to do.

Think of it from this perspective: businesses provide goods and services that cater to people's needs. If your business creates products that fit people's needs and preferences, there will be a higher chance that people will buy your products – because they need it.

So perhaps in thinking of a business concept, ask yourself what it is that you think people need? Please bear in mind that humans are highly complex creatures: they have basic needs for food, clothing and shelter; but they have higher needs: they need to feel empowered; they need to feel in control of their lives, they need to feel accepted, loved and comforted. In defining 'need', you have to think of tapping into what people perceive of themselves and what their hopes and dreams are.

For instance if you meet a nurse, caregiver or store clerk who is on her feet the whole day, what can you offer her that would meet her need and comfort? That nurse, caregiver or store clerk would certainly accept something that would ease the tension and fatigue in her feet, legs and hips. Now, think what craft product you can create to cater to this need? A pair of fleece-lined slippers so soft so she can pad around the house would be good.

One lady thought that since she, a nurse, lived all alone in her apartment, all she wanted was to soak in a warm bath. She thought of buying some herbal preparations to add to her warm bath water to ease tension in her muscles and make her feel silky and smooth so that she can have a good night's sleep. That is one great idea.

Another lady thought that she wanted a handy warm compress she could apply on her feet as she snuggled in bed with mug of tea and a book. She made a pillow, filled it with fine sand, aromatic seeds and herbs. She put this pillow in the microwave for just a few minutes on high and it came out warm. She had for herself a handy warm compress that she can take to bed. Don't you think that is a good idea?

Personal needs can be turned to business ideas

Another lady who was into photography loved to go out on weekends with her kids in tow. She wanted to have fun with her kids and take pictures of them and the surrounding scenery. With her kids' photos, she could make personalized calendars and Christmas cards and give them away to her relatives. She can also make a yearly newsletter detailing the memorable events in their family and give these away to relatives abroad as a way to keep in touch. These are ideas of business concepts that she can use to make her hobby a business venture.

She could start a service making newsletters for other families to detail their activities. They can order as many newsletters as they wish to send to their relatives for Christmas. But let's say that as she got more involved with her photography, she decided to invest in a really good (and expensive) digital camera. Her problem was finding a sturdy and yet trendy bag to store her camera while she travelled with her kids on the weekends.

She tried to find one at the mall but all they had were the standard camera bags. Wherever she went, she was always looking out for a good camera bag but couldn't find one. She was frustrated that she could not find a practical bag that protected the sensitive camera against moisture and mishandling and yet still look stylish. The bags she found were either practical but not stylish at all or stylish but not practical or sturdy at all. Her frustration led her to decide to make a bag for herself. When her friends saw her bag, she got compliments for it. None of her friends could believe that she made it herself. Her friends were into photography, too and boy, did they want a similar bag. They became her source of ideas for other designs. They became her source of inspiration.

That became the concept of her camera bag crafting business. She decided to put up a small single proprietorship for the purpose of producing bags that were functional and fashionable. She set out to make bags that were sturdy and hardworking, big enough to be able to carry accessories like chargers, power cords, extra batteries, lenses, cleaners and other paraphernalia she would need on photo shoots. She especially thought that her bags should look stylish enough to pass for a ladies' purse so that thieves will not suspect that the bag contained an expensive digital camera.

First Things First: What's in a Name?

With the business concept defined, it was time to find a catchy name. What should you name your company? The name should embody your identity but also hint at the concept of your products. You can use your wits and be as wildly creative as you can. Be descriptive and yet precise. Be whimsical and yet comprehensive. Choose the best words that encapsulate who you are and what your products are all about.

Make sure that your business name is unique. You do not want to infringe upon another company's business name. You could get into a world of legal trouble if you do. If you have come up with a name but you are not sure if it is unique enough, you can try to Google the name and see if there are other crafting companies that bear the same name that comes up in the search. You can also try to Google the product description and see what kinds of company names come up. For instance, in that example about the camera bags, you can search the term 'camera bag' or 'ladies' camera bag'. Look at the names and see how you can avoid copying, imitating or even sounding like any of them.

You can always use your own name, for instance: 'Patricia's Practical Photography Purses'. It can be a mouthful but that name immediately gives the customer an idea what your product is, what your business concept is and what makes your products unique. Note that the name 'Patricia' can be your name (you're lucky then, because that name also happens to be the name of an elite and rich class of people in Ancient Rome – rich can also mean elegant). 'Patricia' can also be your dog's name if you're into dog purses (you know, the little purses that fit everything a woman needs including her toy Chihuahua).

If you register your business (and you should, really), you can actually ask to reserve a name and the business bureau in your locality can search their databank to see if that name is available. If it is available, you can reserve that name by paying a small fee. The reservation fee can usually be offset from the registration fee you will pay when you finally decide to register your business. You will usually be given a period of time to register your business under that name. So, you can have time to decide whether you want to stick with that name you've come up with or think up another name.

Do you need a logo?

As with any successful business name, the goal is to have name and product recall. You want your crafting company's name and its logo to go together like peas and carrots or bread and butter or spoon and fork. The name and the logo work together like peas and carrots because they are striking in color contrast but they also need to be like bread and butter: one is nothing without the other. Your name and logo must also complement each other like a spoon and fork. The name must be heavily identified with the logo and vice versa.

You can also register your business logo along with your name. You can design the logo yourself free-hand (since you're artistic as you are a crafter). You can also use a computer-designed logo. Just like the business name, you want your logo to be unique. You can check with the business bureau in your area to see if there are any companies with registered trademarks or logos like yours.

Other considerations:

Inventory and self-analysis

If you are having trouble coming up with a business concept, perhaps you should begin with assessing, first of all, your strength as a crafter. What kinds of craft products do you love to do? What kinds of craft techniques are you most adept at using? Which of the craft products that you've made are popular gift items? Which craft products have you made that got you the most compliments? Sometimes, you need to follow your gut instinct as to which product you should go with.

Perhaps you already have a number of products. What you need to know is if these products have a market. For this you need to see if similar products on the market sell as well. You will need to realistically compare your products with the products available in the market. If yours need improvement in quality so that it can compete, then you must spend time and effort in improving your product. If your product is superior in quality (my hat off to you), then you will still need to evaluate the market to see to a different approach in selling your products. For this you need to do what is called market research.

Value of Market Research: What Is Out There?

If you're still not convinced about which product to make your standard bearer, perhaps you should browse the internet or take trips to local craft shows and craft fairs to see what products are out there. If there are market days in your area, go to the local market and see the variety of products there are. From this, you can gauge if there is a glut of the same type of products you intend to manufacture and market, or, if you find that your products are unique -- you already have that unique product you can build your business on.

Do you remember when a game application on touch capacitive smart phones became all the rage? You could go to a flea market and find stall upon stall filled with items with red, blue, black and green birds. You saw them on T-shirts, on pillow cases, lunch boxes, tote bags, notebooks, pencils even key chains and key holders. They were just everywhere. If you create a craft product with similar characters on them, you can ride a popular trend. You could also get into legal trouble for copyright and trademark infringement. And besides, trends are short –lived. Other game applications become popular after a while and eclipse the popularity of these characters. In fact, about a year after those birds flew the coop, a group of yellow pill like creatures took their place. You can ride the wave of the popular characters but your products will not last in the market after the popularity of the trend wanes. You want to develop products that will last and endure the superficial whims to become items that people will always need and desire to purchase.

You can check out what other people are selling and you can observe what items sell best. You can mark the type of craftsmanship and the quality of goods that are out there and see if your level of work is up to par with those. If your level of craftsmanship is not yet as good as those which are readily available, consider taking crafting classes or downloading crafting ideas from the internet. Do not be afraid to admit when you do not know or understand something. You learn best when you know what you don't know.

At community centers in your area, there may be craft classes and small business ideas. There may be church groups and other micro-entrepreneur groups that give classes on soap making, beading, jewelry making, candle making, basic cookie baking and candy making among other things. You can attend these classes because they usually give pointers as to where you can source raw materials that you may need. They can also assist you in finding specialist equipment that you may need.

If your level of craftsmanship is superior, well, then, you can think of ways to improve on the design and quality of the products you see before you. Use your critical eye and look at ways to improve the product and make it unique. If you were going to buy the product right in front of you, what things would you look at to satisfy yourself that you will receive a product that gives true value for the money you pay for it? Ask yourself why you wouldn't buy it. These kinds of questions can help you in developing your own product.

Ask questions from the seller. Crafters are often eager to share their love for their craft. You won't need to pry. You can be just another interested buyer. You can ask about the materials used and say that you are worried if it is non-toxic to your pets or to small children. Ask if the paint is lead-free. Ask the compounds that make up the product. Ask if they are environment-friendly. Ask about the smallest details until you are sure that it is a good product. If you are sure that it is, ask yourself if it is worth your time and attention to make a similar product. Ask yourself if you can put your thinking cap on and make a better product than the one before you. Think of tweaking and improving existing products. Think of niches in the market you can sell the tweaked and improved product.

Here are some ideas

- If you're into beading, for instance, you can always purchase beads from suppliers. There are all sorts of beads: some are plastic, some made from wood. There are shiny ones and ones printed with numbers and letters. They come in all shapes and sizes and they can be used to make hair accessories, jewelry, brooches, purses, belt buckles and even belts. Beads can also be used as decorative accents on a variety of products.

- You can make soap from natural products such as oats, citrus fruit, olive oil, fruit and floral essences and even milk.

- You can make scented candles in different shapes and sizes. You can make them in different colors and you can add perfume or essential oils to give them a unique scent.

- You can make hair accessories such as headbands, bandanas, pony tail holders, barrettes, hairclips and even tiaras.

- You can make small personalized needlepoint canvases for newlyweds with their names on it and the date of their marriage and have these framed as wedding gifts. You can also make cross-stitch canvases for newborns with the date of the baby's birth. This can also be framed and hung in the nursery or baby's room.

- You can make trinkets that can be used as lanyards for cell phones or other handheld gadgets.

- You can make covers and cases for tablet computers that can also double as a reading stand for them. The covers can be made of leather, or of silicone. It can be personalized with a metal plate engraved with the owner's name and address on it.

Market bias

There is a problem when you do develop your product based upon pure market research such as this, though. That is, if you develop a product that is similar to products out there, you won't be innovating. What will make your product unique is the innovation you can introduce. If you choose which craft to concentrate on based on what's out there, you might be catering to what others perceive as products needed or desired by a market that has already been defined and developed by others. Those kinds of markets may already be saturated. Entrepreneurial trailblazers know how to identify the need of a certain market niche and develop a product based upon their perception of that need.

If you look into yourself and put yourself in the shoes of the ordinary housewife, professional, student or teenager, you can project and extrapolate what they might need. You can look at people's habits and preoccupations and create a product to meet their need, or else, create a product that can enhance their convenience. You can ever really know what a potential buyer would need until you put yourself in his shoes.

You must ask yourself: what kind of people frequently visits this store or market? Are they housewives on a budget? Are they housewives with disposable income? Are they professionals looking for a product that meets a need for their peculiar line of work? If you focus your observation on things people need or what they might need, you might come up with a different and, more importantly, a unique product based on your own personal assessment and definition of the market. Who knows? You might even create your own market or you might corner a market that no one has ever thought of before.

Your unique perception

No two people can look at one and the same object and remember the exact same details. Each person uniquely interprets what he sees according to taste, experience and personal preferences. Who knows but that your taste, experience and preferences may lead you to create a product that other people with similar sensibilities and needs as yours may find attractive. These people who share similar sensibilities as yours may find your produce so necessary that they can easily part with their cash to acquire your product.

Since you are a unique individual, you can certainly use your unique powers of perception to find a market, create and develop a product specifically for that market and corner it. You might actually surprise yourself – you might not only be a crafter, you might also be an innovator.

Think, think, think! Unique doesn't always mean new

When we talk of product development and developing unique products, you don't necessarily have to invent a new product. You can always tweak and twist an old product to make it uniquely functional and uniquely appealing to a certain market. For instance, oven mitts are necessary kitchen items. Every single housewife and home cook needs a good pair of sturdy oven mitts, right? Have you tried buying oven mitts lately? What kind of oven mitts are there out there? At the mall, at specialty shops, at the markets and on the internet – what kinds of oven mitts are available. Choose which one you might buy and analyze what reasons you have to buy it.

Will you buy this pair of oven mitts because of the print? Would you buy it because it was thick and plush? Would you buy it because it protects not only your palms but also your forearms? Would you buy a pricey pair of oven mitts if it was made of fire-retardant material? Would you pay more for oven mitts that have a non-slip grip? Are they thick enough to provide insulation and protection for your hands? Are they too thick that it makes it difficult for your hands to be agile? How about the fit? Do they come in sizes or is it one-size-fits-all?

Can you sew them so that they have a better and snugger fit inside? Can you sew oven mitts that give a better grip? Can you improve on the colors? Can you improve on the materials used? Can you improve on the design of the material used? Polka dots, stripes, checkered and plaid are ordinary designs. Can you make them in neon colors? Can you sew on the cook's name?

When we talk about a 'unique' product, the product does not have to be new. It does not have to be an original invention – it can be an improvement on an invention. It can be an addition to an invention. It doesn't have to be rocket science, it doesn't have to be groundbreaking – but it must be one-of-a-kind. For this, you can take a common item and tweak and twist it so that it can be your take on a common everyday item that breathes new life and usefulness to the common every day product.

Be aware of trends and needs

Cell phones are all the rage these days. Everyone has one. Even if they are easily available, they are still items of value that you need to take care of. They contain information that you need for your business or personal life. It contains numbers of friends, relatives, business contacts and network contacts. You cannot lose your cell phone, drop it or misplace it. So what if you want to go for a walk but you are also waiting for an important call? You want to go out for a walk but you don't want to be cumbered with a purse or a backpack. You just want to bring your cell phone but your outfit doesn't have pockets or you do have pockets but these are not deep or roomy enough for a cell phone. What do you do? You can create a cell phone carrying case, of course.

You can design one that can be worn around the neck – your cell phone can fit into that case and you can wear it like a pendant or you can tuck it under your shirt or jacket and thieves would be none the wiser. You can put your phone on vibrate mode and when you feel it vibrating, you can duck into a store or phone booth and answer it there. You won't get mugged for your cell phone and yet you are sure that your cell phone is accessible when you need it.

There are a million and one cell phone cases in the market, right? So what kind of cell phone cases can you craft that will be attractive, practical and functional? How can you design a cell phone case that can be unique? Think of the trends in cell phones – people usually use smart phones now with a big screen. Perhaps you can design a smart phone case that is protective and one that allows the owner to use the smart phone without removing it from the case. That way, the phone is protected from moisture and from damage if you suddenly drop it.

Unique Products From a Unique Process

Often, the question is not whether you can create a new product. Often, the question is about creating a new technique or improving upon an existing technique or process that can spell the difference between an ordinary product with a' really good' product. By a 'really good product' I mean one that you would buy for yourself, buy for the members of your family or even give away to friends and staff at the office and recommend to your friends and colleagues at work.

Let's say your product is a common everyday household item like coasters. There are plastic, metal and wooden coasters. What if you can develop a product that takes the existing materials used and add to it so that your coasters can retain the heat or cold from the drink that is placed on the coaster. Perhaps what will make your coasters unique is not the material but a new technique or process of using temperature-retaining substances which will render your coaster a one-on-a-kind product that appeals to a unique market. Perhaps adding or cladding a layer of porcelain or enamel to the metal or wooden coasters can help absorb and retain the heat or the cold temperature from the cup or glass that is placed on the coaster. Now that would make your coasters unique, won't it?

If you understand something about science, then you understand that sometimes the temperature at which a product is heated alters the properties of the material. Added heat or lowered heat or slowly increasing the heat or blasting the heat may make the material more brittle, more malleable or more elastic. Each new technique in processing the material can be registered as a separate copyright. You are not going to register the formula of the material (that is probably covered by an existing copyright or patent already) what you can register is the process or technique that you've developed if the process or technique is new and it consistently produces the desired result.

If you copyright or patent your process or technique, each time that another company wants to use that process or technique, you can be paid a royalty for its use. This way, you not only have unique material by which to make your unique product, you can also have the exclusive right to use the technique and others who may have a mind to use the technique you developed will have to pay for that right. You earn from your craft in two ways: from the sales of the product using the material you've developed from your new technique or process; and also earn from licensing the use of the technique or process.

Finding suppliers and raw materials

Part of market research is finding suppliers who can provide supplies and raw materials reliably at reasonable prices so that you can produce your craft product cost-effectively. You must have a steady and accessible supply of raw materials for you to be able to produce your products. You can always use the internet for these types of inquiries.

The one big issue about ordering from the internet is the reliability of the supplier to ship and deliver your supplies on time. You will want to do business with a company that takes your business needs seriously even if your orders are small. You want good attentive service that encourages you to cultivate a good business relationship. You must also find suppliers who can sell you raw materials at a price that will allow you to maximize your profits.

Choosing a supplier from another country may not be such a good idea unless the raw material you need is simply unavailable locally. Shipping would be a major concern. T he cost of shipping may jack up the production cost of your product. The shipping cost would also depend upon the speed at which the items are delivered to you. You may also have to check with the local laws and ordinances in your area if the materials you may need may be the subject of higher tariffs or taxes if obtained abroad as opposed to obtaining it locally. Quality and value are the primary consideration in finding suppliers.

Maybe the crafting idea you have can use materials available in your own backyard. This is preferable than sourcing supplies from abroad. Your production cost will be a fraction if you can find materials for your product from your own garden or backyard.

Some women in a rural area who were living next to a river saw the overabundance of water lily plants. The water lily plants were a nuisance as these got caught in the propellers of boats and barges. The plants also trap trash which impeded the waterway and raise the risk for flooding. The women decided to 'harvest' the water lily plants and tried to see it can be used as extenders for livestock feed. Some of the water lily stalks became really tough when dried that they found it could be used for rope. The rural women experimented with the stalks and one decided to make baskets out of the stalks. And, just like that, they had a steady source of raw material for making baskets and bags. They learned weaving and designing techniques for making stylish bags, purses and even window blinds and other home décor. It just goes to show that there could be cash in trash and one man's trash is another man's source of cash.

Look around your neighborhood. Look for things that you have you got in abundance that no one seems to have any use for. Think of ideas and ways by which this 'trash' item may be used to produce products that people want to buy.

Other women worried about the environmental impact that shiny plastic foil-like packs for juice drinks may have. They seem to always end up clogging the sewage drains. They decided to pick those up. They were sturdy enough and did not easily tear. They tried sewing them together and because of the regular geometric shapes of the plastic foil juice packs, they could be sewn into tote bags or reusable grocery bags. Plastic straws can be folded up, knotted and strung together to make flower arrangements or curtains.

There are so many things you can make out of discards. They are not only good for the environment as gathering and reusing these products save up space in landfills, they are also good for your pocketbook as the materials you need to make your products cost next to nothing. Look around you. You might just find something that no one has ever thought of using before. You might just hit upon a really good idea for a product that will sell.

Sourcing Capital for Your Hobby Venture

It might do well to stop for a while and think about capital sourcing. Where will you get the money to begin this craft business? Will you get it from your personal savings? It might be smarter to start small. A few hundred dollars to start with can make you enough money (and then some) so that you can use the earnings from that small capital and add it up as more capital.

You can borrow from friends and family, of course. You can even give them a share in the profits (instead of paying interest on the personal loan). You can ask your friends and family to contribute a small amount from which you can create a pool of funds to start with. Whatever profits you realize will be distributed to your friends and family until the amount they added to the pool has been returned to them.

You can always hold a garage sale and the money you realize from the garage sale can be your start-up capital. You can raid your house for recyclable items (aluminum cans, PET bottles, newspapers, old books and notebooks, etc.) and sell the recyclables to junk dealers. Don't be afraid to start small. Giant oaks begin as acorns. Your business can grow even if your beginnings are humble.

Apply for a micro loan

You can always apply for a personal loan. There are a lot of non-government organizations whose advocacy is in helping ordinary people become entrepreneurs. There are foundations whose mission is to fight poverty by encouraging entrepreneurship. They are willing to train and encourage small entrepreneurs in starting a business.

They can train you in the basics of starting a business, keeping your books and financial records accurately, filling up government forms for income tax and social security payments. They can also help you find sources of capital for your small or medium scale business from micro-investors. There are a lot of incentives and tax breaks that governments give to small and medium scale businesses such as crafts. This is in line with encouraging economic development and growth at the grass roots level.

What Next? How To Explode Your Sales

So now that you have capital, your company has a concept, a name, a logo and you've registered as a business, you have developed a product using your own crafting expertise. You have settled upon materials and equipment you need and you've found a reliable source for these items. What next? You must work to introduce your product in your target market.

Create a buzz

Open an account on a popular social networking site. Take pictures of your products, make a brief write up about them and share them with your friends. If they are truly your friends, they will sample your products and give honest (and, hopefully favorable) opinions about your products. These are called blurbs. If they are willing, photograph your kids and your friends wearing or using your craft products and post their blurbs along with their photos. Discreetly provide your company's contact details. If you can add the price for your items, it would be much better.

Wouldn't it be so much easier if your customers on the internet can just pay up in cash? Yes, in an ideal world, it would be so much better. But you may have buyers from places far away (that's the beauty of the reach of the internet). You might want to set up a long distance payment scheme through one of the online payment services. You can register as a merchant or you can register an account under your own personal name. Most of these sites allow you to register for free so that you can receive payment for free but they charge you a small processing fee (around 10%) when you make withdrawals from the online payment service to your bank account. You must check these things out.

You might want to put up an account on an online market. You can creatively register your products under several categories so that there will be bigger chances for your products to be seen by people browsing the online market sites. For instance, if you are selling mobile phone carrying cases, you can register them under the category of ladies' accessories but you can also register them under fashion accessories, wallets or mobile phone accessories.

Your community or church group may have a newsletter or bulletin board. You can ask if it is possible to place a small advertising flyer in the newsletter or post it on the bulletin board. You can always post a flyer on the community billboard at the grocery store or community center. If your children are raising funds for a yearbook and they are selling spaces for advertising, take advantage of these advertising opportunities. You can also place ads in the local paper or locally published magazine.

Some local television shows and television stations often make a top ten list of gift giving or gift-making ideas for holidays. They also air segments on local specialty shops or local specialty products. They also run shows with human interest stories. If your crafting business has helped unemployed housewives or high school students gain income on the side and improve their lives, you can be interviewed for local TV. You can advertise your advocacy and your products. You can flash the contact numbers of your company where viewers can place orders.

Use your products and be your own endorser

If you have kids, give a few of your products to them for them to use in school where other kids and other moms can see them using it. If your kids have show and tell, your kid can discuss how to make the craft products. If they have math fairs and they put their new math skills to use by selling items from a booth, why don't your kids sell the products you make? You can pay them a commission for each item they sell. Doing this helps you hit three birds with one stone: your product is introduced to a market for free; your kids learn how a business works; and you get to make some money.

A lady had a daughter with lovely hair. She decided to make hair accessories for her daughter to use in school. With a glue gun, beads, buttons, sequins, ribbons and small wooden letters, she made headbands, scrunchies, clips, ponytail holders and barrettes. First, she made them with her daughter's name on it. Then she made them with her daughter's best friend's name on it and gave it to her to use.

Her daughter gave them away to her friends for Valentine's or as party favors when she invited her friends over for her birthday party. Next thing she knew it, her classmates wanted to buy hair accessories from her. That lady had a sales agent in her daughter. Her daughter made money to buy stuff she wanted and she was learning the value of money, hard work and running a business. Her daughter was also a good resource for what was 'cool' to the kids at school.

The mother and daughter craft entrepreneurial team put up booths at school fairs and donated a bit of their earnings from their sales to the school. When her daughter needed to raise money for her club at school, she sold her mother's craft products at a small mark-up. The mark-up went to the fund raising effort. Part of the profit was given as commission to her daughter. A percentage of the sales was also donated to the club.

Package deals

One lady started her craft business by making little keepsakes for her niece to give away to the ladies who attended her engagement party, bridal shower, her wedding and her baby shower. Her niece's friends took notice of the craft items and ordered some to give away to their friends who attended their own bridal shower, wedding and baby showers. Soon word of mouth grew. She began to make an inventory of products which could be personalized with the date and names of the newlyweds or the babies. Then she started entertaining orders or made to order craft products that her customers wanted for their own occasions. Her business grew by word-of-mouth.

She started networking with event planners who made her craft products part of their 'package deal' for events. She expanded to corporate giveaways for Christmas. First, she used her own craft products as gifts to give to her own staff for their birthdays or for Christmas or Mother's Day. Later, she personalized the products with the company's name and logo and gave them away to her loyal customers to thank them for their business. The manager at the company took notice and started ordering her products as company giveaways.

Another lady made specialty soaps, went to bed and breakfasts around the countryside and offered her products as part of the complimentary toiletry packs that they give to their patrons. She also left a few packs on the front counter for the patrons to buy on their way home.

Fairs, bazaars and trade shows

If you cannot yet afford your own shop to sell your products, you have to go on the road and join craft fairs and bazaars. These are good places to introduce your products. Each city or town has a local market day where local products are sold. You can put up a booth at these markets. One day a week for each market town is a good start.

There are also seasonal bazaars, fairs and night markets. Every summer, there are state and county fairs. At Christmas time, there are Christmas bazaars and fairs. On the fourth of July, there are parades and lots of people in public areas. Why not put up a booth to sell your products?

Take advantage of seasonal demands

You might also consider directly selling your products especially around the holidays. If your products involve home décor for Christmas or other holidays such as Halloween, Memorial Day, Mother's Day, Father's Day, Valentine's Day and Easter, you may consider taking advantage of the high demand for gift items for those holidays.

If you are a weekend entrepreneur and you hold down a day job at an office, on your lunch break you can always gather your office friends and show them the gift items they can purchase from you. If you know personal assistants who do the shopping for their celebrity bosses, you can also sell directly to them. People working at an office often do not have much time to shop around for gifts that they want to give away for holidays, birthdays and family occasions. Bringing your products directly to them may not only give you direct sales, you can even be at the right place and time to take orders. Others make the round of offices and offer to collect payment for their products on payday. Or better still, arrive at the office to offer your products on payday itself.

You may also consider taking advantage of your contacts at churches and charitable organizations which do a lot of gift giving and assembling of care packages as gifts to give away at orphanages, foster homes, and elderly homes. If you offer them a good price, they can buy wholesale from you and include your products in their gift packages for the less fortunate. This way, you create buzz for your products, you can make minimal profit and help the community.

Never underestimate the business you can generate from joining state or town fairs. Especially if your craft product uses indigenous materials or locally sourced raw materials, you can certainly put up a booth at a state fair as part of enhancing pride of place and promote the locally produced products while earning money as well.

Why not start a club or class?

There is strength in numbers. There are so many people who desire to learn new skills. You can invite people to join a knitting club and you can supply them with starter kits and teach them how to knit. You can volunteer to handle a quilting or knitting class at a community centre and offer to sell supplies to the registrants. You can charge a basic fee for the class and include a starter kit as part of the basic fee. If you don't want to teach a class, you can approach a person who teaches such a class and ask if you can help by making starter kits available for the students. You can give the teacher a share in the profits.

If you crochet or make jewelry, you can create a club and sell not only jewelry making kits but finished products as well. You can help people learn new skills and help them create designs. You can charge a fee for attending the class and you can charge for the materials and supplies.

Some people want to learn things but they simply do not possess the talent, perseverance or diligence to follow through and finish a project. When they become frustrated, they just might think of merely buying ready-made products instead of making them. Be prepared to sell items you have already made.

You can invite a locally renowned expert to give a lecture. You can organize the lecture, charge a fee and also put up a booth to sell your products to people who will attend. You can even ask others who are also selling their crafts to put up booths around the seminar or lecture area. Only make sure that your lecture has a theme or concept and the crafters who will exhibit their products follow the concept or idea of the lecture or event.

You may also sponsor a demonstration. People are interested in the products if they can see how it is made. People also want to learn and witness new techniques and new processes in creating products. If you can arrange for a demonstration at your booth, you may actually attract an audience and make a sales pitch for your products.

Along with your craft products and supplies to create similar products, your demonstration booth can also display tools and implements for sale. For instance, if you arrange a knitting demonstration, you can sell knitting needles along with the knitted items. You can sell threads, yarns, scissors, rotary cutters, cutting mats and all other items which customers who buy your craft products may also be interested in buying for their own use at home.

Consider blogging about your products

If you are a mother whose child raising experiences has led you to create a product that most mothers would need, you may consider advertising your products by creating and maintaining a blog. You can advertise your products and help give mothers out there necessary information on common childhood ailments, allergies, safe educational toys etc. You can blog about any of your experiences that other moms can relate to and advertise products that assisted you through that experience.

You can blog about how you learned how to make your product. You can blog about a problem or situation that spurred you to come up with an idea that has become your advocacy and business as well. You can blog about how you managed your time and balanced your energies and attention to raise a family, develop and market a product and engage in business. You can blog about anything under the sun and use the blog post to advertise your products by providing links and badges on the leaderboard of your blog. Ask a knowledgeable and internet savvy teenager or computer geek for help to set up the blog and set up your links.

Partnering and Networking

It makes sense to partner up and network with others in a related line of business. For instance, if you make wicker baskets and hampers, you can probably partner up with stores that sell gourmet gift hampers. You can provide them with the baskets where they can package their products.

If you make scented candles, you can partner up with a friend who makes aroma therapy oils and soaps. You can package your products together and offer them as gift items for mothers on Mother's Day. You can find spas and offer to sell the items on consignment at the spas.

If you make organic gourmet jams, jellies and fruit spreads, you can always sell them on consignment to small country hotels, bed and breakfasts or roadside cafes. You can sell it to them for them to use as items on their menu or display the jams, jellies and fruit spreads near the counter where the customers can buy them to take home.

If you sell knitted Christmas tree ornaments you may consider partnering up with a company that sells Christmas trees. At a mall, you can probably lease temporary floor space to put up a booth or kiosk where you can put a sewing machine or embroidery machine so that you can personalize items that you sell. For instance, if you sell Christmas stockings to put small presents in, you can offer to sew up the name of the person to whom the stocking will be given.

T-shirt printing is also popular as holiday gifts and you can partner up with a professional computer designer who can create designs for shirts. Professional choirs and sports teams often like to go to official functions in club shirts with their name and the name of their group on it. Some high schools have annual homecoming reunions for their alumni. They might want a souvenir shirt with their name and the school's logo on it. You can partner up with a person who makes shirts or partner up with a person who makes decals and together, you can offer these products and services.

Business cards, flyers and tarpaulin billboards

It makes sense to have business cards and flyers printed. The business cards and flyers may contain photos of your products with the prices. They must also contain your contact numbers and website or email address. You can post these on community billboards. You can give them away with free samples outside grocery stores or at sporting events.

If you decide to put up a booth, make sure you decorate your booth to make it attractive to buyers. Make sure that your logo and company name is easily seen and read. Make sure that even the bags you use to wrap your products in contain contact numbers for your company. Always put in a flyer or a business card when you wrap the items that have been bought and paid for. That way, the buyer can always contact you for more orders.

When to Consult Professionals

It is always good to consult professionals when you need help to set up or register your business or make it more attractive to customers. When should you consult a professional? Do not wait until you feel overwhelmed and frustrated or when you are already slapped with a complaint or a violation. Knowledge is power. If you need information and specialized knowledge that you can't get off the internet or read from a book, then you should consult a professional.

Web Designer

If you intend to create a website for your products, you need a professional web designer who can set up your website and make it attractive as well as functional. You will need to create banners and badges that can be used as links or advertising at social networks. Even if you only intend to create a webpage on a social networking site or on a sales site, it will still help if a person who knows what he is doing can help you display photos of your products, your company logo and company name.

You may need help designing and creating an electronic greeting card or flyer by which you can offer your products. You might need to create an email list and automatically send electronic flyers announcing new products or promotions to the names on the email list. You may need a person to set up the flow of email inquiries that land on your website so that you can easily and promptly be notified of emails you need to reply to. For all these services, you need a good web designer.

Accountant

You will need the advice and assistance of a certified public accountant to help you register your business for taxation purposes. You will need to prepare financial statements, profit and loss statements and other financial records. You will need to keep a ledger where every single transaction is recorded. There are software programs that can help you keep your financial records, but just the same when you submit and file these with government revenue offices, your financial records must be accurate and they must conform to the accepted accounting formats. For this, you will need the services of a certified public accountant.

Lawyer or Solicitor

If your business involves health inspection and certifications from health boards, you may need the assistance of a lawyer. If you need to register a copyright or a patent for your products or for the techniques and processes you have developed, you will need to draw up papers proving your ownership and creation of the process or technique. You may need help in filling out legal forms to register your business or your ownership of a copyright or patent. You may need to submit sworn affidavits or statements. You might need advice before you enter into and sign contracts. You may need to write letters of demand or letters of complaint. For all this, you will need the services of a solicitor or lawyer.

Realtor

If you are thinking of putting up a shop or business premises, you may need the help of a realtor who can find a suitable store or shop for you. There may be zoning laws to comply with that will restrict the places and areas that can house both a sales shop or store front and also a manufacturing area. You may want to convert your garage into a workshop or factory. You may need special permits for these and a realtor can help you with this.

Financial advisers

You may need help in sourcing funds. A financial adviser or consultant can help you analyze loan products and loan facilities that can help you in the long term. You may need ideas to find funding and how to invest the funds wisely so that you can maximize the capital you have raised. You can ask for help in restructuring loans or in settling a debt by making a payment proposal. You can also ask help from a financial adviser so that you can learn how much of a profit margin you need to keep your business afloat. You can ask help to trim down overhead and operational expenses.

Labor consultants

If your business picks up and the work load can no longer be met by you, your spouse, your children and your next door neighbor you might find yourself needing to hire workers. Whom can you hire? What compensation packages can work best for you as a small business that is just starting? What sort of documentary requirements do you need to submit to register your workers for social security, health care and other benefits? How can you properly be a withholding tax agent so that your worker's salary can properly be deducted for taxation purposes? How can you work our work shifts and schedules?

Do you need an employee's manual? Do you need to draw up company rules and regulations? Do you need employment contracts drawn up? What should these contracts contain? These issues can be clarified for you by a labor or human resource consultant. As these issues often spell litigation for unfair labor conditions and practices if you fail to comply with labor standards, it will do you well to avoid these headaches by starting off on the right track and consulting a labor expert.

If you decide that you will pay your workers a piece rate for every product they finish making, how can you make sure that the piece rate pay you give them conforms to the requirements of minimum wage? You can ask a labor consultant to devise a time and motion study to determine how many pieces can be manufactured within an hour to determine how much you need to pay your workers so that their piece rate work can approximate the minimum wage standards mandated by the law in your area.

You can also determine if it would be better to hire independent contractors to make the job. You may need to know the difference between employees and independent contractors. In the first place, independent contractors offer skilled labor and services based on talent or creative skill as only artisans have. Also, independent contractors have and use their own tools, implements and machinery to do the job. An employer does not have control over the manner by which an independent contractor makes the product unlike the control and employer can exert upon an employee. An independent contractor usually does not keep regular hours at the workplace. He can work at home or at his own atelier and merely bring the finished products for quality control at the place of business of the owner. These are issues that a labor consultant can clarify for you.

Another issue that you may need help with from a labor consultant is in the firing of employees. Not all persons you hire have a good fit with your company's culture. Sooner or later, you may need to let some of your employees go. You will surely need help in figuring out what causes you can cite for firing your employees. You will need help in drafting notices of termination and in making sure that you pay your employees all their benefits. You will need the counsel of a labor consultant so that you can insulate and defend yourself against complaints.

What It Takes To Go Big

Perseverance

Realistically, even with an excellent product, you might not make huge profits at the start. You might incur debt and you might be lucky if you break even. It may take some time before your business starts to make a return on your investment of talent, time and money. What do you do in the meantime? You must persevere. You must keep at it. Never let up and never give up if you believe in yourself and in your product.

Quality control

Most craft businesses that begin with a roaring start often end up with a whimper because they cannot maintain the quality of their products. Some find it difficult to maintain a steady source of supplies. Some find it difficult to find cost-effective sources for the materials they need. Others are consumed with the idea of making a fast back and they take short cuts. They scrimp and save on materials by substituting them with cheaper ones. There is nothing wrong with trying to bring down your overhead costs so that you can make profits. Others try to pare down the overhead and production costs instead of raising prices so that they can remain competitive. But do not do this at the expense of the quality of your products.

Always remember that by the time that you register profits, you would have made a name for your company and you have established a reputation. This is called goodwill. Your goodwill is your company's reputation. People expect that your products will maintain its high quality through time. And you must do your best to protect your company's goodwill.

Protecting and maintaining your goodwill does not mean that your products should remain the same all throughout. The quality must be maintained but the products must be diversified and developed. Your products must evolve to meet new needs and societal challenges. You must also innovate with the same energy that you used to develop your products.

Diversifying and innovating

To diversify means producing other products that may be similar or related to your other existing products. It may mean creating products that have different features or different styles. For instance if you develop baby booties, you might introduce booties with rubber soles or booties in different colors or with different materials. It may also mean introducing matching socks with the booties. It may mean producing bibs and hats that match the socks and booties. This is what diversifying means.

Innovating means that you add new lines of products. In that example of baby clothing, you might branch out and develop products like pull-up toilet training pants for toddlers, jackets that help toddlers learn how to work buttons, zippers, snaps and buckles to learn how to dress themselves. You can also branch out and develop new products that 'grow' with the original market for which the original products were developed.

It may also mean developing products that help children learn to read, recognize letters, count to ten and generally help them develop their cognitive skills to prepare them for school. It may mean developing products that toddlers may need as they prepare to start school such as snack bags or backpacks. It may mean developing toys that help children develop their gross and fine motor skills to enable them to learn how to write and manipulate tools like scissors.

You must apply the same tenacity and creativity in creating these new products to add to your line. You can attend exhibits and trade shows so that you can analyze the trends and technological advances that can help you innovate and diversify your business.

Final word on corporate social responsibility

You began your business because you wanted to turn your dream into a profit generating business. You wanted a creative outlet for your artistic or technical flair and you wanted the challenge of creating products that people need and want. It felt good to be your own boss and to make money from your talents.

You have been empowered by your venture to direct your own career and professional life. You are making your own money. The next question that you must face is, how can you give back to the community? How can you empower others and inspire them to also realize their dreams of owning their own businesses? This is called corporate social responsibility and it entails giving back to the community that helped you nurture your talents by nurturing the talents of others.

This book has recounted the experiences of ordinary men and women with extraordinary courage, talent and diligence. It seems appropriate to end this book with a story of empowerment. In a poor neighborhood, some women made extra money by weaving strips of cloth into area rugs. The strips of cloth are discards purchased from garment manufacturing factories. The women knotted the strips so that they formed long strips that can be fitted on a wooden board that had nails pounded on it. The nails are the anchor for the strips that will be woven. The women mixed and matched the colors to make the area rugs attractive. The women made three to five area rugs per day and they were paid a pittance for them.

Some students who were doing outreach feeding programs in the poor neighborhood noted the women's occupation and decided to train the women to start their own business. They taught them the basics of sourcing the cloth for themselves and cutting out the middleman so that the women can earn more for their area rugs. The students organized seminars for the women to teach them new techniques and new designs for the area rugs.

Soon, the women began creating and marketing their own area rugs. They formed themselves into a cooperative and they split among themselves the earnings for all the area rugs they sold themselves. They have since branched out into creating other woven products. The women from the entire neighborhood belong to the cooperative. They share the tasks. Some women design, others weave, still others source the strips of cloth and others market and sell the area rugs.

Those students who helped the women in that poor neighborhood have since tried to duplicate the same business model in other poor neighborhoods. They ask the women to speak before other women in other neighborhoods and they have assisted in training other women from other neighborhoods.

They have become empowered. They earn a good living from creating products they can be proud of. Their products have been entered in design competitions and they can be found in specialty stores in malls. They give back to the community by training other women. It has become their advocacy to help other women to empower themselves. Their earnings have allowed them to start a play school and early learning center for the neighborhood children.

The lesson in corporate responsibility is that it pays to invest in people and in communities. You will reap good things by sowing good things. When you've realized your dreams and found fulfillment, help others realize their dreams and also find fulfillment.

We Want Your Feedback on This Book!

Our main purpose is to make sure that our readers get value from the books we publish and that they have a good experience with all of our products. We are always working to improve our books and other products with every revision and update.

Every piece of feedback makes a difference in this process. And we would appreciate yours as well - whether it is good or bad.

Please take one minute to let us know what you thought by following this link:
http://checkmatemg.com/feedbackcrafts/

www.ingramcontent.com/pod-product-compliance
Lightning Source LLC
Chambersburg PA
CBHW071541170526
45166CB00004B/1508